Key Stage 1

Mathematics Revision Notes

Authors
Penny Coltman
Jayne Greenwood
Valerie Mitchell

Letts
EDUCATIONAL

First published 1999
Reprinted 1999
This edition 1999

Letts Educational,
9–15 Aldine Street, London W12 8AW
Tel. (020) 8740 2270
Fax. (020) 8740 2280

Editorial, design and production by Hart McLeod, Cambridge

British Library Cataloguing-in-Publication Data

A CIP record for this book is available from the British Library

ISBN 1 84085 327 1

Printed in Great Britain by Ashford Colour Press

CONTENTS

CONTENTS

INTRODUCTION

Working through these revision notes will help your child to feel confident in maths. They will also help you to understand some of the ways in which maths is taught at Key Stage One.

The book is divided into clear sections, each dealing with a different area of maths. In each section you will find:

- an explanation of the maths covered
- ways in which you can help your child to learn and remember the maths
- activities which practise the maths.

Remember that little and often is the best recipe for success. Give plenty of praise and encouragement and remember that the golden rule is to stop when it becomes clear that your child has 'had enough'.

Number

COUNTING

This section describes ways of helping your child to count. It is important that children can count objects, record the count as a numeral and recognise the number when it is written as a word.

How you can help

- Practise saying the names of numbers in the correct order; one, two, three, four, five and so on.
- Sing nursery songs and rhymes with number words during daily activities; travelling in the car; playing at bath time; walking in the park.
- Start with numbers to five or ten, gradually introducing larger numbers. Most nursery rhymes such as '5 speckled frogs' or '5 currant buns' count backwards. Although all counting songs are helpful in developing number awareness, keep a special lookout for those which count forwards, such as '1, 2 Buckle My Shoe'.
- Count objects, saying one number word for each object.
- Find situations in which you can count actions, such as climbing stairs, stacking bricks or even just clapping or stamping.
- Playing simple 'track' board games will also help in counting.
- Make sure that your child can recognise all the numerals from 1 to 9.

Only count as you 'jump' the counter along the track; one jump, one count.

- Talk about how we use zero, 0, to mean nothing or none. We don't have a special numeral to represent the number ten, but use 1 and 0 written together.
- Practise recognising number words.
- Make a set of cards with number words written on them. Encourage your child to practise reading them and matching them to numerals.

Counting in rows

Use rows of real objects to practise counting, encouraging your child to touch each object as she counts it.

Count these rows of pictures together, touching each picture in turn. One touch – one number.

It is helpful to count from left to right.

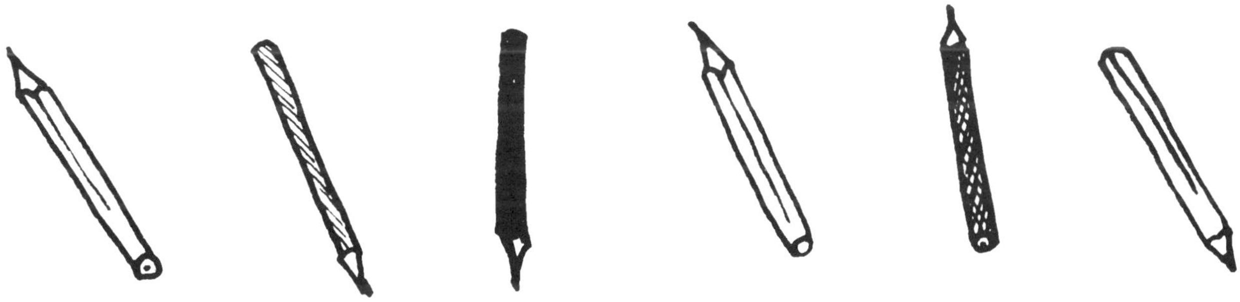

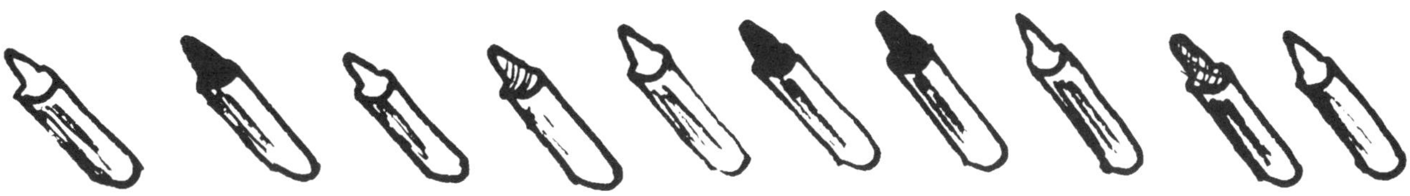

Counting grouped objects

Now try counting some objects which are not in rows.

Start by placing some objects on a table or tray so that each can be touched or moved in turn.

Then try counting the things in each of these sets.

Counting to a total

Find a collection of objects for your child to count. Suitable ideas would be small plastic toys, spoons, pasta shapes, shells, leaves, or conkers.

Ask your child to count out a given number of objects.

Once your child can confidently make sets of up to ten objects, encourage her to draw given numbers of objects, such as spots, worms or shapes.

Encourage your child to move the objects to one side as she builds her counted collection.

Counting beats

Play the Clapping Game

Ask your child to listen carefully whilst you clap your hands. Can he copy exactly what you do?

Count aloud as you clap two, three or four times and then allow your child to copy.

Talk about counting 'in your head'.

Matching quantities

Find the pairs of sets which contain the same number of bumble bees.

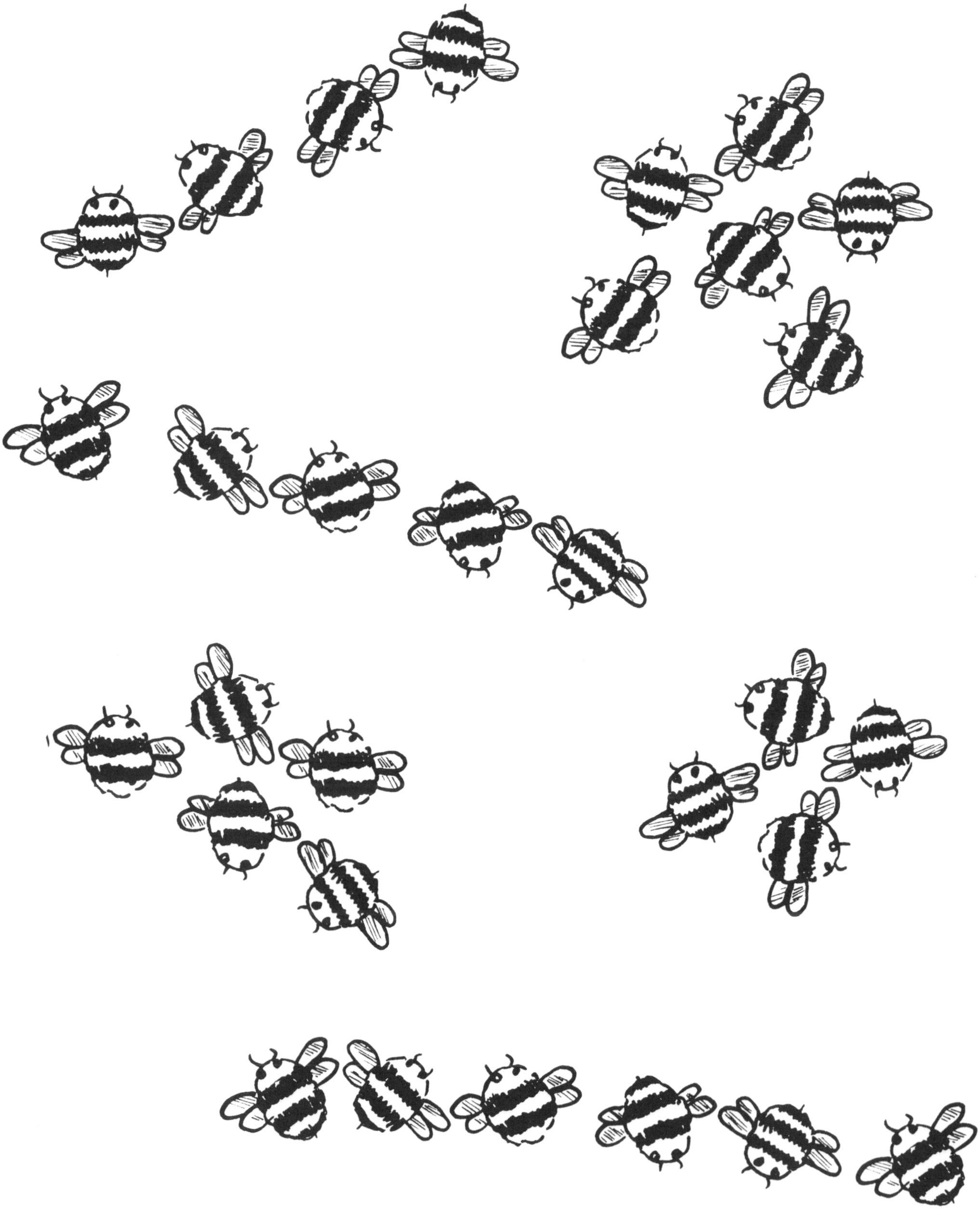

Recognising numerals

Look for numbers as you go for walks, in books that you read with your child or spot them on television programmes.

Make a set of cards with pictures of objects, and another set with numerals.

Play a matching game

Can your child find the correct numeral for each set?

ACTIVITY

Reading number words

Children will be able to recognise and read number words a long time before they are able to write or spell them.

Add to your card game by making a set of number words.

Now the game is to find trios: sets of objects, number words and numerals.

6

five

four

six

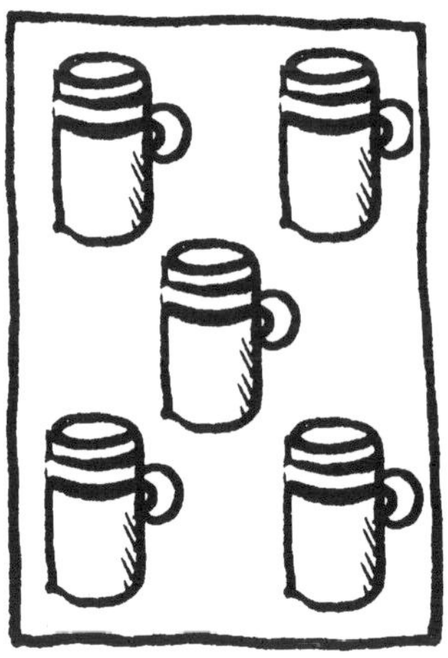

4

5

ORDERING NUMBERS

In this section your child will practise ordering objects and numbers.

How you can help

- Place a few groups of pasta shapes on the table. Ask your child to say which is the largest group and which is the smallest.
- Use words such as more, less, fewer, most, least, biggest and smallest to help your child to develop the language used for comparing numbers.
- Make a row of toy animals and talk about the first, second, third and fourth animal in the row. These words are called ordinal numbers because they describe the order of objects, ideas or events.
- As you are doing jobs at home ask your child 'What is the first thing we need to do?' or when making decisions: 'My first idea was...'
- Hold teddy races and make rosettes for the winners.
- Use toy cars to make a long traffic jam. Which is the first car in the jam? Make a set of cards with the numbers 1st, 2nd, 3rd, 4th and 5th. Use the cards to label the cars in the traffic jam.

- Hold teddy races and make rosettes for the winners.
- Make a pretend car park by laying books or magazines on the floor. Each book is a parking space. Count the spaces from left to right. Now give instructions: Put the red car in the first space. Put the blue car in the second space and so on.
- Jumble the instructions:

  Put the yellow car in the sixth space. Put the lorry in the second place.

  Ask questions such as 'Which car is in the tenth space?'

Ordering pairs

Place some groups of objects on the table, or use these pairs of pictures.

For each pair, ask your child to choose the larger set.

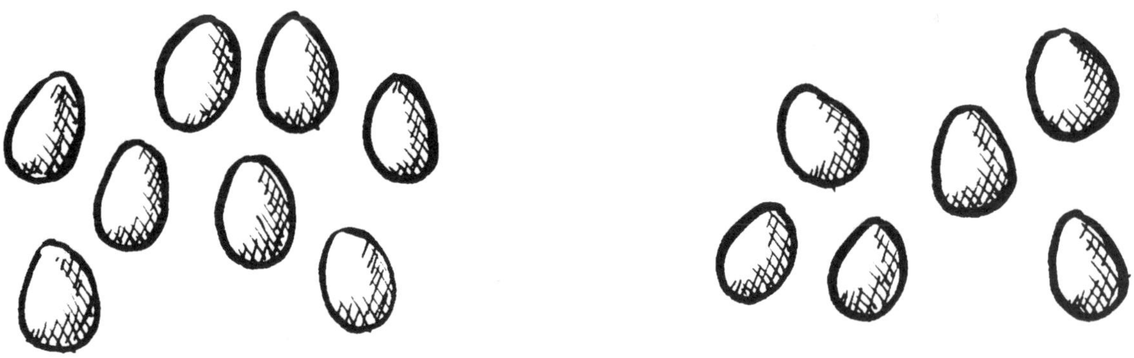

Ordering groups

Make a set of cards with the numerals 1, 2, 3, 4 and 5 on them.

Use familiar materials to make sets of one, two, three, four and five objects.

Ask your child to count the number of objects in each set and to place the correct number card with each set.

Now ask your child to tell you which set of objects has the most things in it? Which has the smallest number of things in it?

Can your child put the sets in order from smallest to biggest?

Use these pictures to reinforce the idea. Start by asking your child to record the number of objects in each picture.

Talk about the largest and smallest sets of ice creams.

Which set has the most?

Which has the least?

Can your child put all the sets in order from least to most?

The jungle race

Tell your child a story about a race held between the animals of the jungle.

Here is a picture of the end of the race.

Ask your child questions about the race.

Who came first?

Who came second?

Who came last?

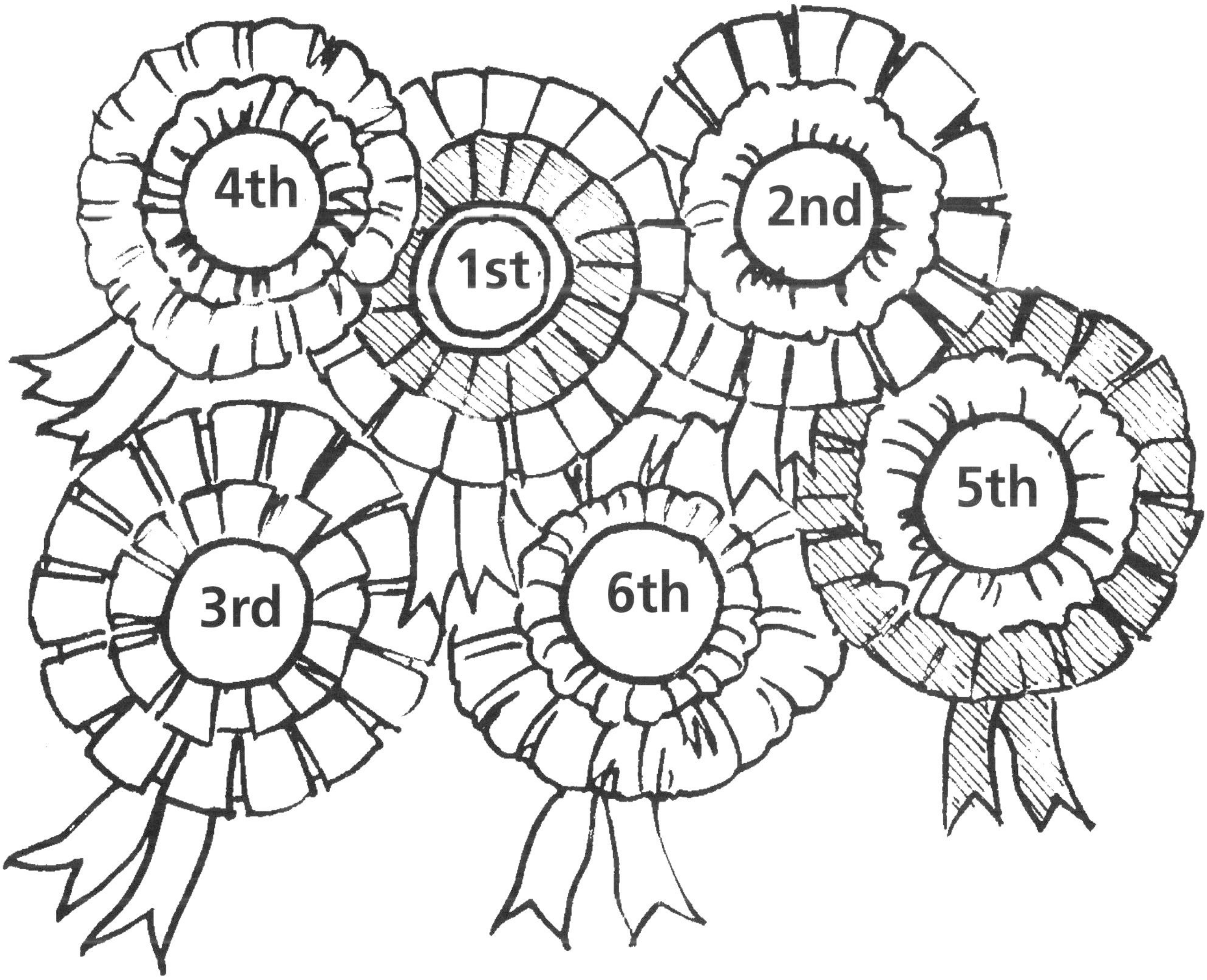

Explain to your child that rosettes are often given to prize winners.
The rosettes are usually different colours.

Ask your child to find the rosette which says 1st. Colour it red.

Find the rosette which says 2nd. Colour it blue.

Find the rosette which says 3rd. Colour it yellow.

Find the rosette which says 4th. Colour it green.

Find the rosette which says 5th. Colour it pink.

Find the rosette which says 6th. Colour it purple.

Which rosette should be given to each animal?

Snowmen on parade

This page will give plenty of practise in using ordinal numbers. See instructions on page 17.

Your child will need a pencil and some crayons.

Read these instructions aloud for your child to follow.

Point out the ordinal numbers written in words as you read.

Give the second snowman a red hat.

Give the tenth snowman a broom.

Give the sixth snowman a blue scarf.

Give the third snowman an orange, carrot nose.

Give the first snowman a row of buttons down his tummy.

Give the fourth snowman a yellow hat and a green scarf.

Give the ninth snowman a black, coal nose.

Give the seventh snowman a stripy scarf.

Give the fifth snowman a spotty hat.

Give the eighth snowman some twiggy hair.

For confident children:

Find the snowman which is between the fifth and the seventh one.
Give him a bobble hat.

Find the snowman which is next to the tenth one. Give him a long, bright scarf.

Finish the activity with some questions, encouraging your child to use ordinal numbers as they answer.

Which snowman has a broom?

Which has a stripy scarf.

Which ones have no hats?

ADDITION

In this section your child will practise the skills of addition.

How you can help

Introduce addition in a play situation.

- Hold a teddy tea party. The teddies are joined by two friends. How many teddies are there now?
- Help your child to add imaginary objects.

  Think of funny situations. Ask your child to imagine two penguins going to a party. One more penguin joins them. How many are there now?
- Introduce a **number line**.

  This is just a line with the numbers 0 to 10 marked at intervals like this:

  Children at school practise early arithmetic by using their fingers to 'hop' along the line as they count or add, just as they do when moving a counter in a board game.

  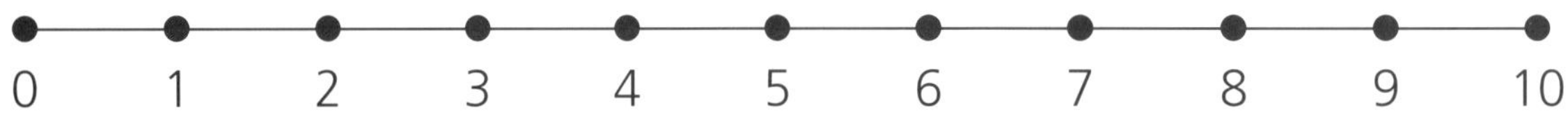

- Use the language of addition so that children learn that there are lots of ways of describing it.

  E.g. plus, more all together, add, count on, the sum of, equals and makes.

  What is two more than three?

  What is two count on three?

  What is two plus three?

  What is two add three?

  What is the sum of two and three?

Number lines

Make a giant number line from old wallpaper for your child to walk along: one step, one count.

Adding two sets together

On a big piece of paper draw two smaller circles and one large one like this:

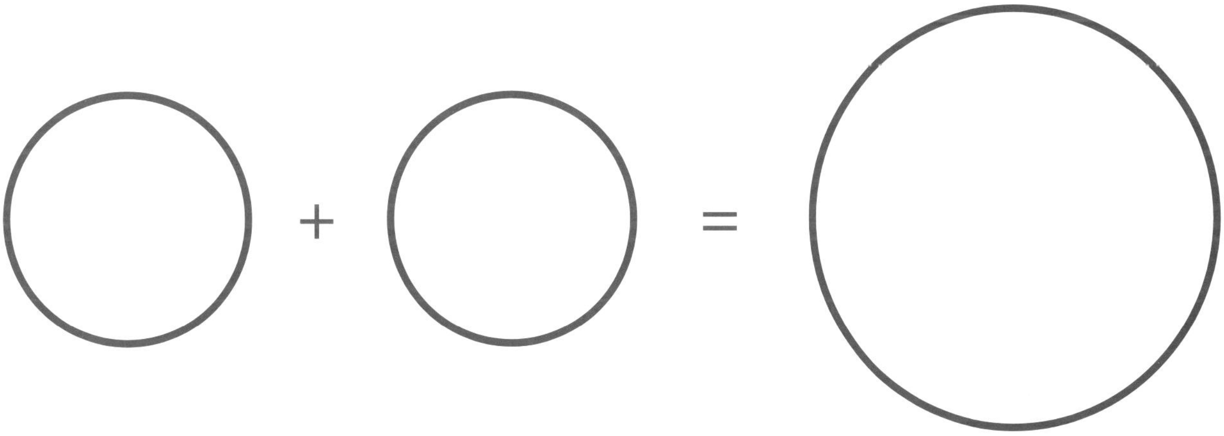

Place three pasta shapes in each of the smaller circles and count them.

Now slide them all into the larger circle and count again.
Record the sum as 3 + 3 = 6

Now try these:

3 + 4 = □   4 + 4 = □   5 + 2 = □

4 + 5 = □   3 + 6 = □   5 + 3 = □

6 + 2 = □   4 + 6 = □   8 + 1 = □

Counting on

Practise using the number line for addition.

Try the sum 2+5. Make sure your child starts by finding the 2 on a number line. Then they count five steps along the line, to the right. The number their finger is now touching is the answer to the sum. This is called 'counting on'.

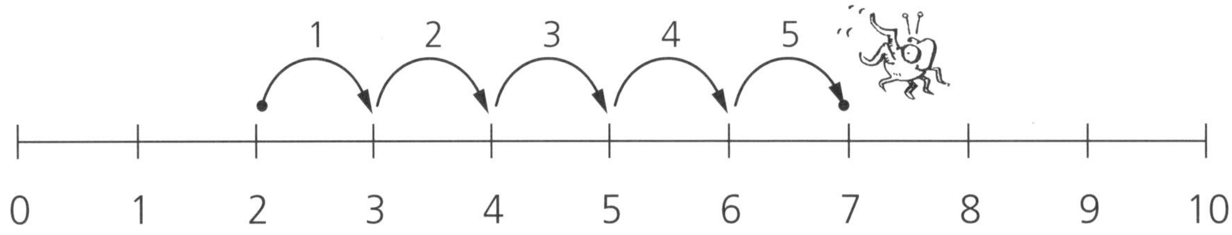

2 + 5 = 7

Now try these.

3+4

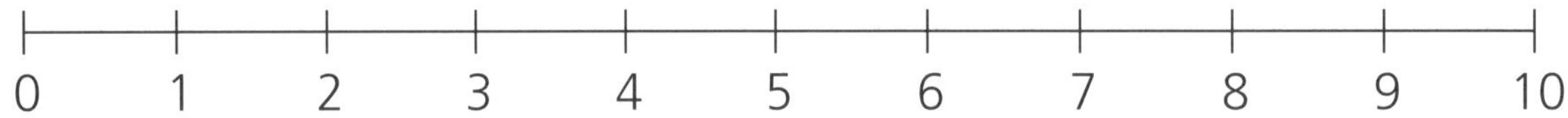

1+6

4+2

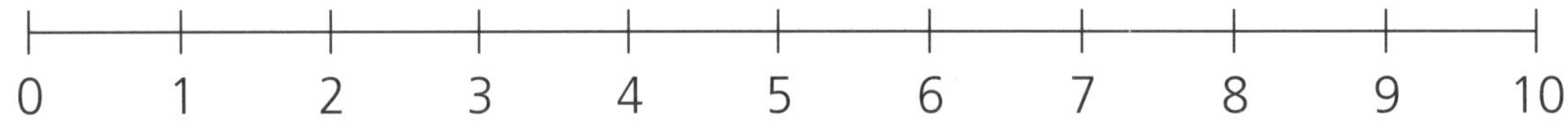

Shape and measure

2–D SHAPES

This section describes ways in which you can help your child to recognise and name various 2–D shapes.

How you can help

- Use familiar household objects to help your child learn the names of 2–D shapes.
- Point out rectangular shapes in bricks, tiles, slates, place mats, envelopes, books, magazines, rugs or towels etc.
- Explain that squares, often found around the house in tiles, napkins, table tops, all have the special property of having four sides that are equal.
- Circular objects can be found in the form of plates, saucers, wheels, pastry cutters, bracelets, saucepan lids, or rings.
- Triangles can be introduced when cutting up sandwiches. Some tiling patterns have triangles cut by halving a square diagonally.
- Other shapes such as hexagons (six sides) and octagons (eight sides) are not so easy to find. Look in children's plastic shape sets or find a game that includes a multi-sided spinner.
- Buy a packet of coloured-paper gummed shapes to reinforce your work. Sort the shapes into various types and label them, e.g. 'A set of squares'. Make a picture with one particular shape theme, e.g. a man made from triangles. Later, make a picture using just one colour but a range of shapes.
- On a journey play a shape challenge game to pass the time.

  Choose a shape and look for an example of it. E.g. Who will be first to spot a triangle?

Naming shapes

Cover the labels in turn. Ask your child to name the shapes.
Colour the shapes in.

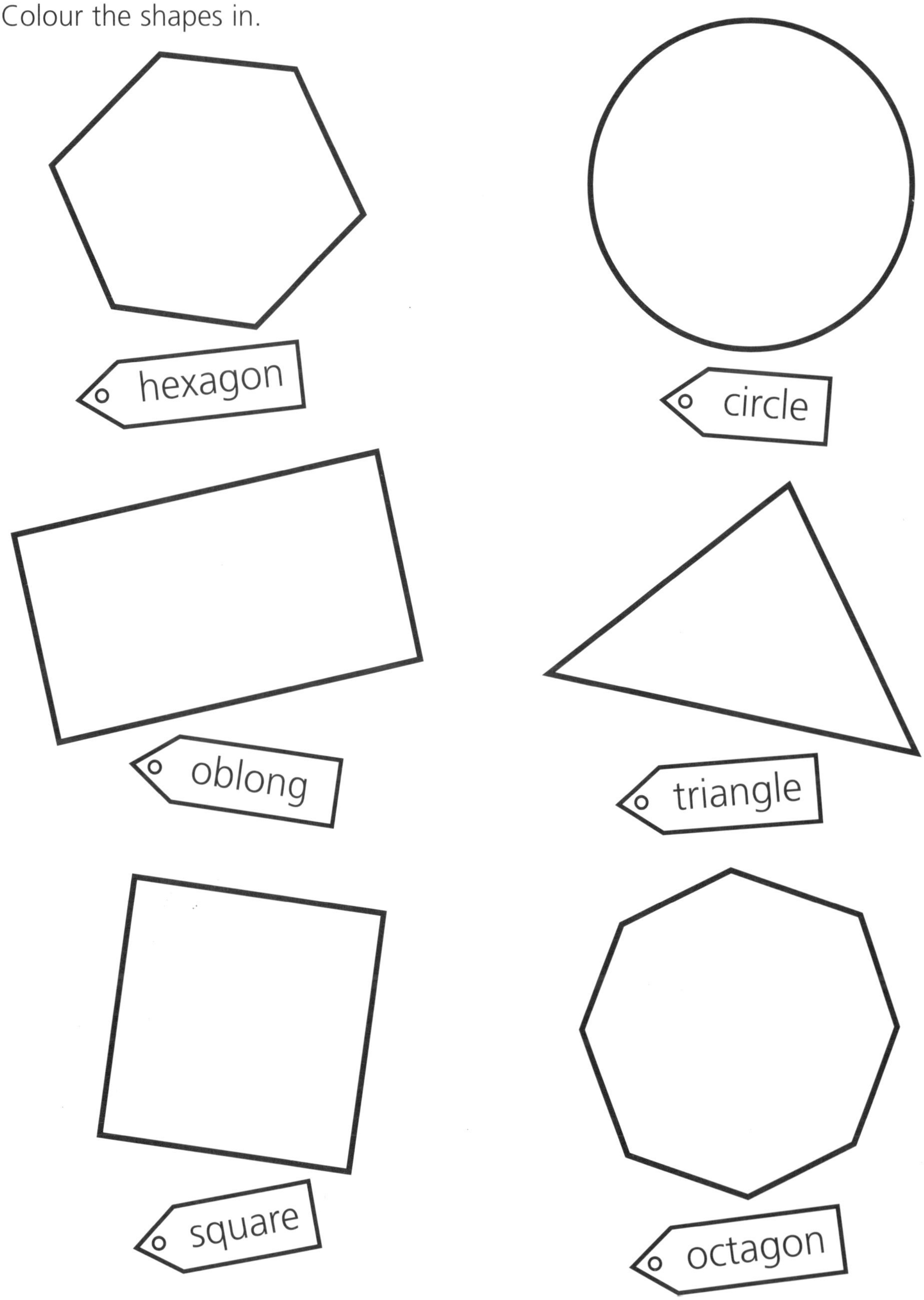

Selecting and counting shapes

Look carefully at the picture and then answer the questions below.

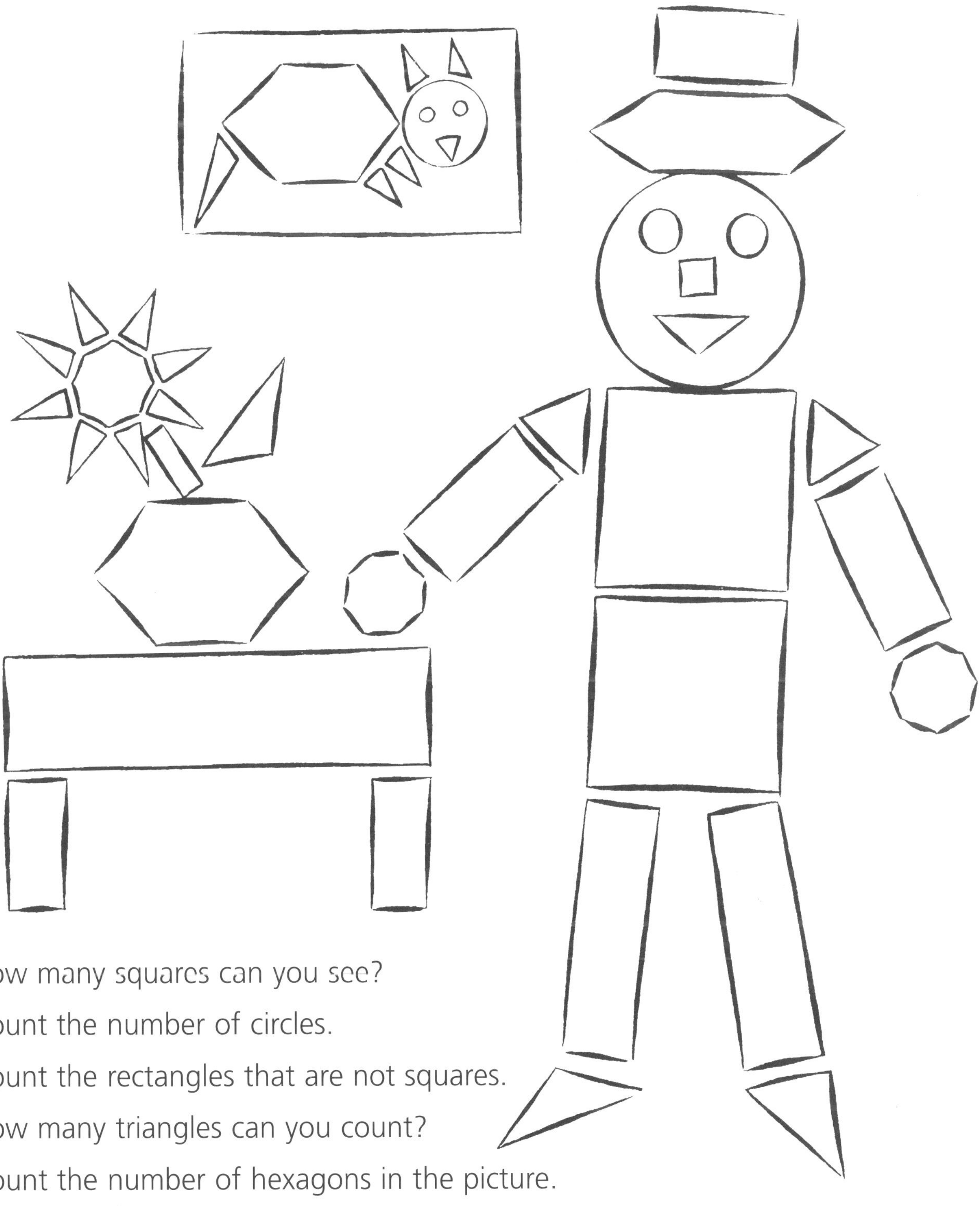

How many squares can you see?

Count the number of circles.

Count the rectangles that are not squares.

How many triangles can you count?

Count the number of hexagons in the picture.

How many octagons can you see?

Colour the picture.

Fitting shapes together

Make a set of cardboard 2–D shapes with about 20 shapes of each type, or use a commercially produced child's shape set.

Use one type of shape to 'tile' or cover the surface of a book.

Encourage your child to make sure that the shapes fit together with no overlaps or gaps.

This is called **tessellation**.

- Explore the other shapes in your set. How well do they act as tiles by fitting together without gaps.
- Which shapes make the best tiles?
- How do circles work as tiles?
- Can you position triangles so that they fit together well? Is there an alternative way?

Use your 2–D shapes to make shape pictures on a chosen theme.

3–D SHAPES

This section describes ways in which you can help your child recognise and name various solid shapes.

How you can help

- Use familiar boxes, shapes and objects that you have around the house to support this work.

  E.g. Cylinders: kitchen roll middles, glue sticks, some sweetie tubes.

  Cubes: some tissue or gift boxes.

  Cuboids: cereal packets, various household boxes.

  Triangular prism: certain chocolate packaging.

  Spheres: balls, bubbles.

  Cones: ice cream cones.

- Use a set of plane (flat) shapes, from a plastic shape set, to develop the idea of solid shape.

  E.g. Help your child to stack rectangles into a pile to make a rectangular prism or cuboid.

  Stack triangles to make a triangular prism, hexagons to make a hexagonal prism, circles to make a cylinder.

- Explain that prisms are regular solid shapes that can be cut into a series of slices of the same shape and size. A loaf of bread is a rectangular prism that can be carved into a series of rectangular slices.

  Not all solid shapes make equal slices, e.g. a sphere or a cone.

  Make rings of different sizes.

- Introduce spheres by blowing bubbles or when playing various ball games. Cut them in half to find the circle family to which they belong.

- When your child is familiar with the names and properties of these solid shapes, play detectives and search the house for objects of a chosen shape.

Naming shapes

Cover each label in turn. Ask your child to name the shapes. Colour them in.

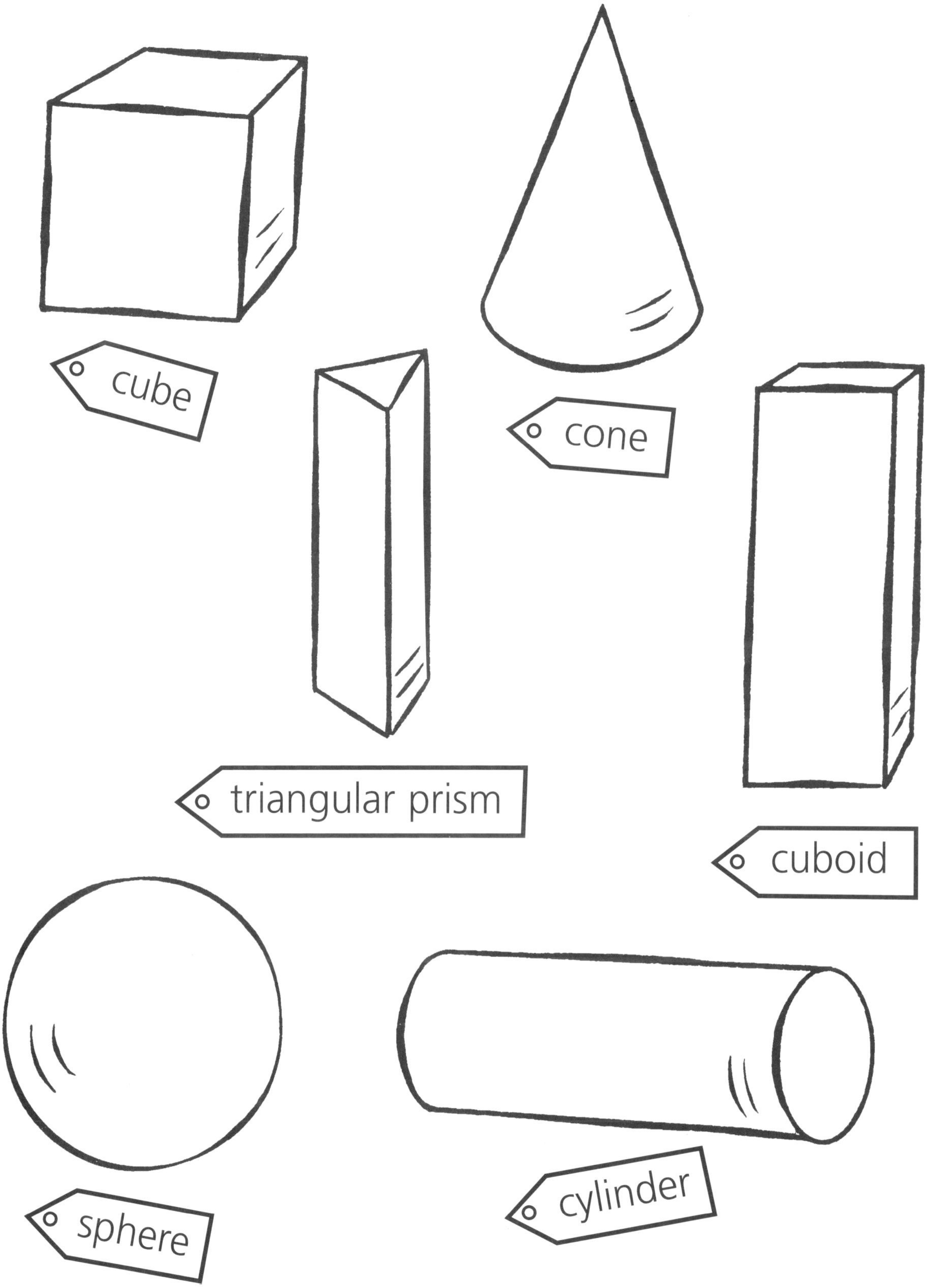

Exploring faces

Find an unwanted cardboard box which is a cube and gently pull it apart to reveal the six squares from which it is made. This flat shape is called the net of the cube.

To help your child become familiar which the number of faces of a solid shape:

Count together the number of faces.

Number the faces with a pen.

Colour the faces using a different colour for each one.

Lay the net onto a piece of paper and draw round it.

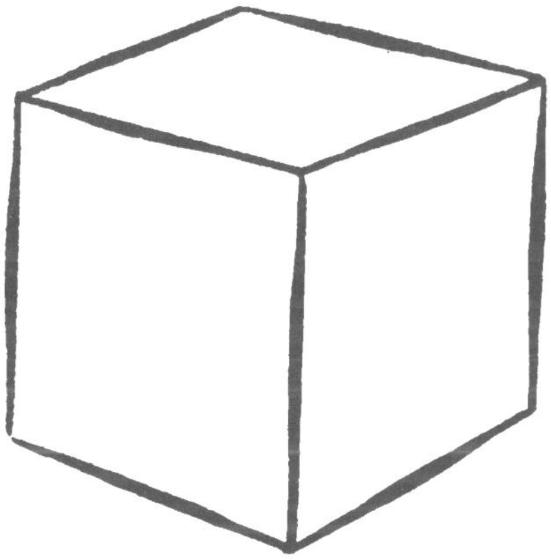

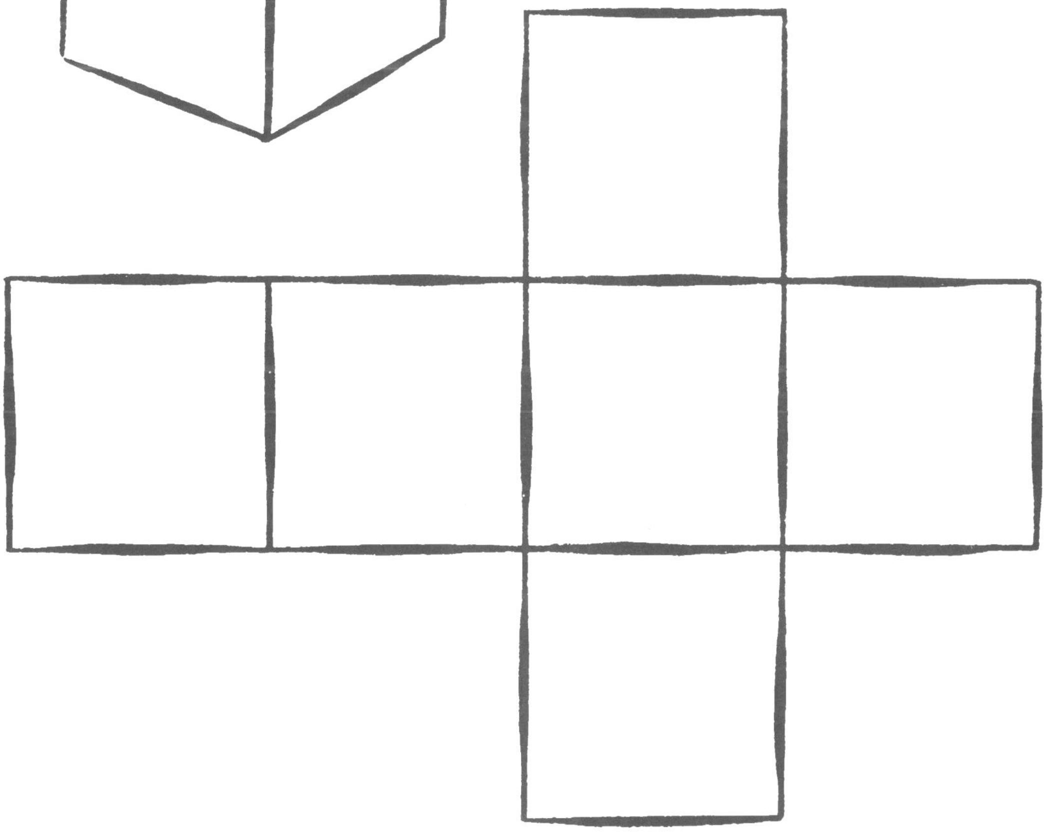

Model making

To reinforce this work on solid shapes make a collection of empty packets and containers.

- These could be used for a sorting activity. Make labels with the names of the 3-dimensional shapes you have collected. Encourage your child to sort the packets and containers into the correct pile.
- Use the boxes and packets to make models. The model could be made of a variety of solid shapes or on one particular theme, e.g. can you make a spaceship out of just cuboids?

FRACTIONS AND SYMMETRY

This section describes ways of helping your child to understand fractions, symmetry and the associated vocabulary.

How you can help

- Explain that the word fraction means an amount that is part of a whole number. Use everyday examples to assist children to relate to this idea. E.g. Divide a sandwich into two parts or halves.

  Cut a birthday cake or pizza into the necessary number of parts or slices.

- Begin with work on halves.

  Using the word half when an object is divided into two equal parts is sufficient at this stage.

  The written notation 1/2 comes later.

- Point out that some objects, pictures or shapes have an obvious line along which they could be divided into halves. Each half is a reflection of the other. This line is called the line of symmetry.
- Look for examples of things that have a line of symmetry, e.g. an outline of a person, a butterfly, a table lamp, some buildings.
- Play at dividing objects into equal parts, e.g. playdough or plasticine, dividing cake mix into cases, folding and cutting a picture into parts.
- Using a balance or scales to see how accurate you are.
- Extend the work on fractions by introducing the words we use when we divide objects into different amounts, e.g. 4 parts are called quarters.
- Play a dividing game with a sheet of newspaper. This is a version of musical chairs. When the music stops the child who stands on the paper folds it in half and then cuts it down the crease. As the game continues, the piece of paper left to stand on becomes smaller and smaller.

The line of symmetry

Look carefully at the pictures below. They have been divided down their line of symmetry.

Try to imagine what the whole picture looked like before it was cut in half.

Now place a small mirror along each dotted line in turn and look at the reflected image.

Draw the completed pictures and colour them in.

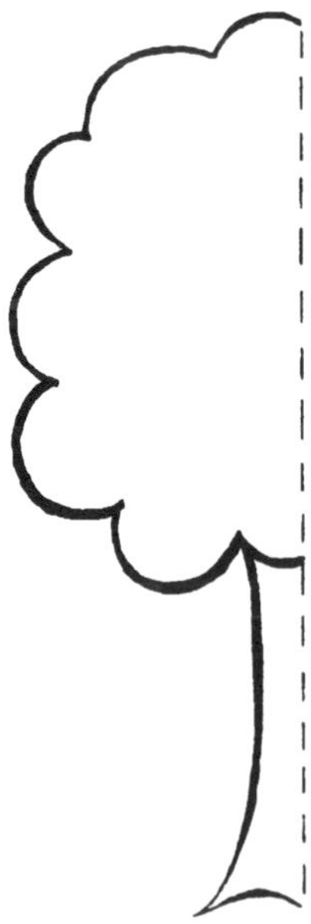

Exploring symmetry

Fold a piece of paper in half and encourage your child to paint half a picture on one half of it.

While it is still wet fold the blank half over on to the painted half and press the paper.

Open the painting for your child to see he has made a symmetrical painting.

Point out that the fold line is the line of symmetry.

Dividing real things

- Use everyday play and household activities to reinforce the work you have been doing on fractions.

  E.g. When making sandwiches or cutting cakes, talk about whether they are to be divided into halves, quarters or more.

- Make a tea party for an even number of favourite toys. Encourage your child to divide up playdough cake so that each guest has the same amount.

Dividing pictures

Cut out regular shaped pictures from magazines and divide into half and then into quarters and so on until you cannot fold any more.

How many parts have you divided your picture into?

- Colour this pizza.
- Help your child to divide the pizza into quarters.

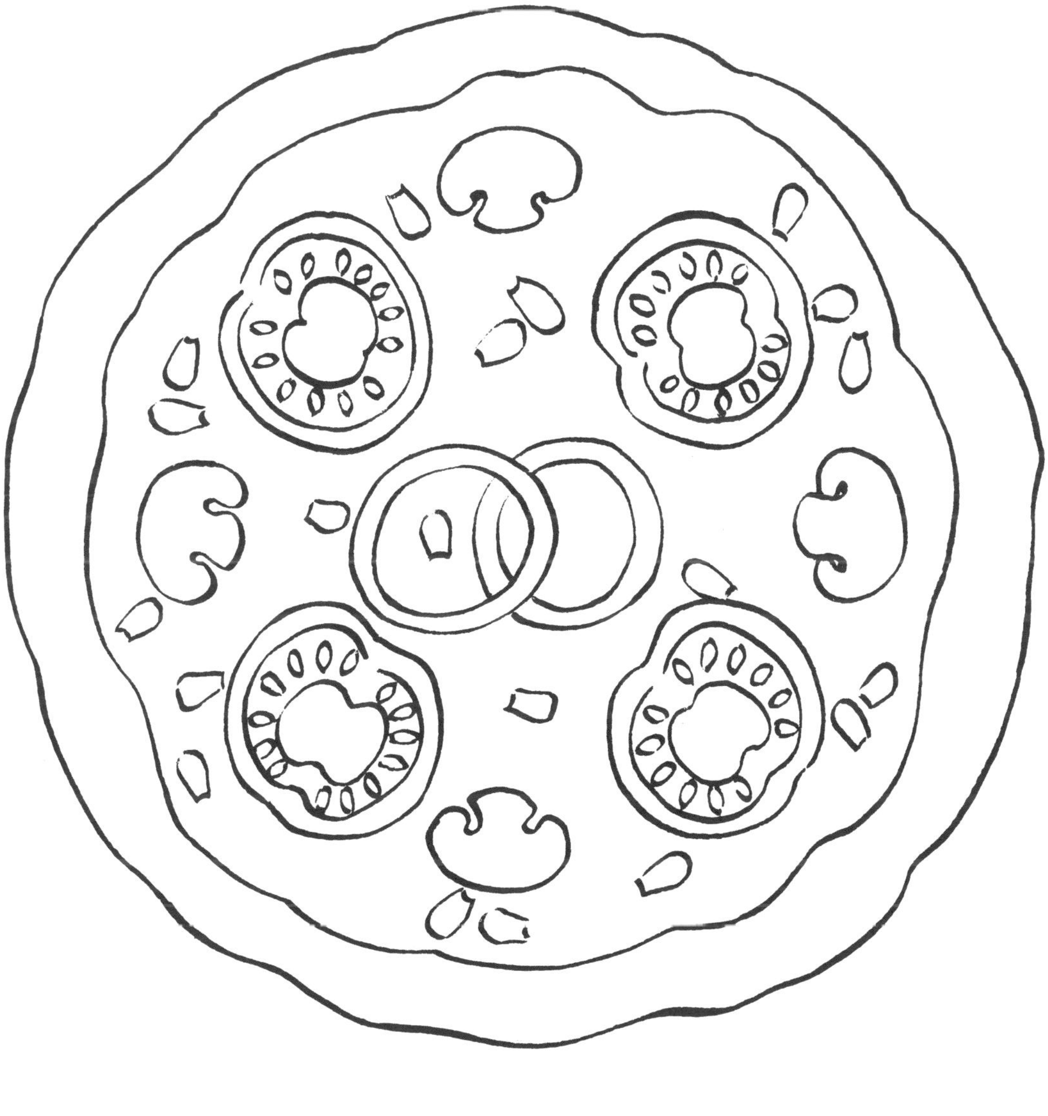

Halving a number

When your child understands the concept of dividing an object into two equal parts you can introduce the idea of dividing or sharing a number.

Start with everyday situations. Ask questions, e.g. 'Two children have four biscuits; how many can they each eat?'

Offer your child plenty of opportunities to 'share out' even numbers of real objects.

Teach them to use little reminders like 'one for you, one for me… .'

Make a challenge game

Use the two identical pictures below and ask your child to add equal numbers of objects to each picture.

E.g. You need six cats; how many are you going to draw in each picture? There are four birds; how many can you draw in each scene?

The child should be helped to divide the number in half and draw half the items in each picture, ending up with two versions the same.

TIME

This section describes ways of helping your child with aspects of time; both measuring time and beginning to tell the time.

How you can help

- Explain that time is broken down into measurable units with different names, e.g. minute, hour, day, week, fortnight, month, season, year. Talk about how these relate to each other.
- Help your child to feel how long a minute is using a cookery or other timer. Set your child a series of challenges to do within one minute. E.g. How many times can you:

  write your name?

  jump up and down?

  count to ten?
- Use everyday routines to reinforce his understanding of the length of a minute.

  E.g. In one minute we are going to read a bedtime story.

  In one minute tea will be ready.

- Extend this to include five minutes.

  E.g. In five minutes it will be bedtime.

  It is five minutes until your favourite television programme.
- Learn the order of the days of the week and the months of the year.

  Use events that are important to the child to help them remember.

  E.g. We go swimming on a Wednesday.

  My birthday is in September.
- Introduce telling the time by talking about the job of each hand on the clock.

  Explain that when the big hand is at the 12 it is always o'clock.

  Give plenty of practice in recognising o'clock before moving on to half past.

Days of the week

Below are the days of the week but they are in a muddle.

Read the names of the days and then write them down in the correct order.

Friday

Monday

Sunday

Saturday

Wednesday

Thursday

Tuesday

Months of the year

Now do the same with the months of the year beginning with January and ending with December.

Telling the time

Look carefully at the clocks below and see if you can say what time they are showing. Write the times.

o'clock

o'clock

o'clock

o'clock

Half past

Half past

Half past

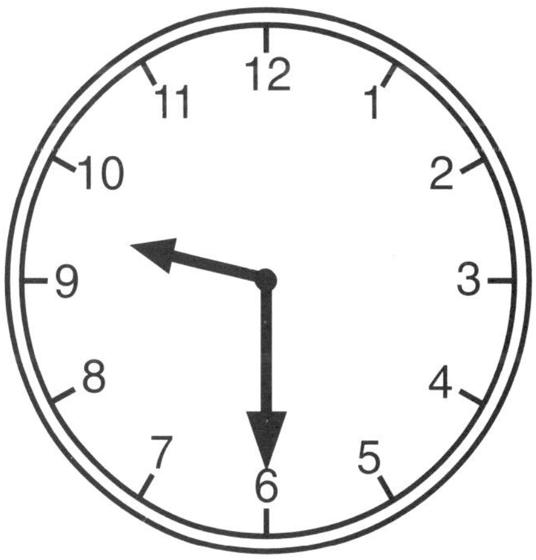

Half past

Working with clocks

Use the clocks to help you answer the questions below.

What time does the pool open in the morning?

How many hours is the pool open for in the morning?

What time does the pool open in the afternoon?

How many hours is the pool open for in the afternoon?

Is the pool open for more hours in the morning or the afternoon?

How many hours is the pool open for in a day?

Handling data

HANDLING DATA

This section describes ways of helping your child to collect, present and interpret data.

How you can help

- Use everyday situations as they occur. When survey results are shown on television or in newspapers and magazines use this as an opportunity to explain that this is a way of showing what has been found out.
- Sort some toy bricks by colour (no more than ten per set).

  Use the edge of a carpet or table as a baseline and lay the bricks out flat in a series of straight lines, one line or column for each colour. This is a simple block graph.
- Talk about the graph that you have made. It should be easy to see which column has the most/least blocks in it.
- Make a set of small number cards.

  Starting with 1 at the bottom, lay them in numerical order up the side of your graph.
- Encourage your child to check the number of blocks in a certain column without counting, by looking for the number at the side.

Making a block graph

Use the 1.5cm squared paper on page 43 and crayons for this activity.

Encourage your child to select a subject on which to gather data or information.

Suitable ideas include favourite foods, football teams, colours, pets and hobbies.

The chosen topic then needs to be broken down into categories and these should be written one per square, along the bottom of the graph.

For example, if you have chosen pets the labels might read rabbit, cat, dog, budgie, goldfish, hamster and guinea pig.

Help your child to number up the left-hand side of the page, with number 1 being immediately above the row of labels (see illustration).

Have fun asking family and friends to choose their favourite category and help your child to record each answer as a coloured square.

Encourage your child to use one colour for each category so that the graph is easier to read.

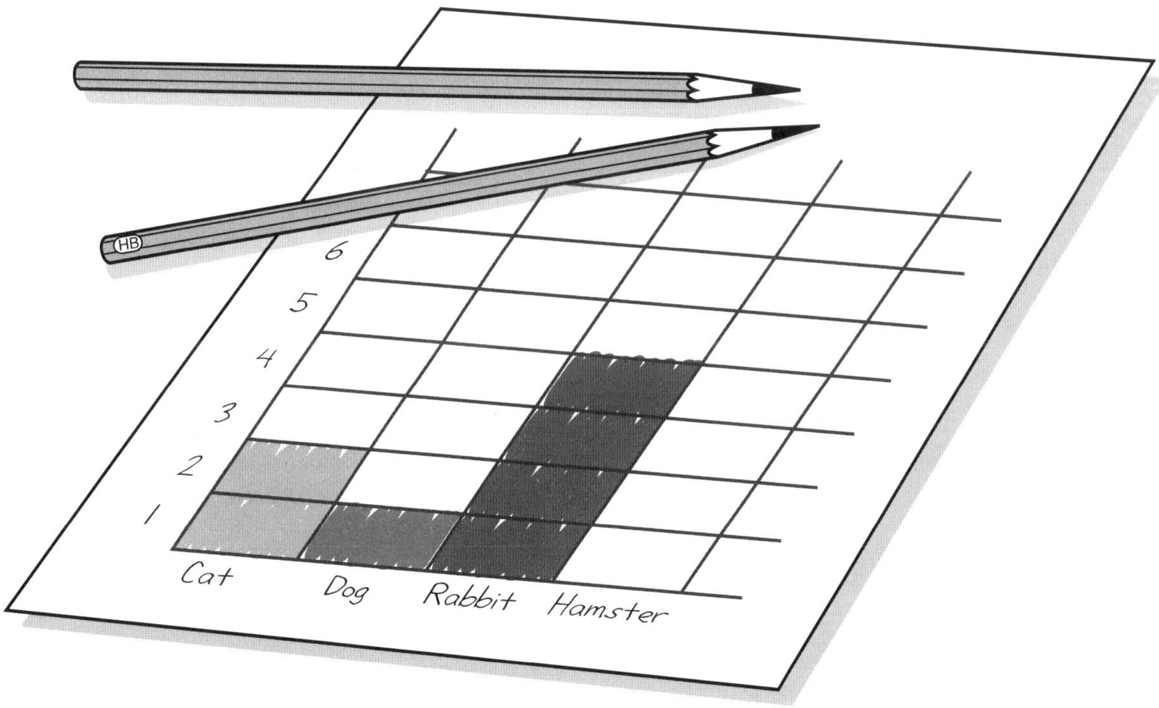

Making a block graph

Interpreting charts

Look carefully at the diagram and then answer the questions below.

	Boys	Girls
Can ride bikes	✓ ✓ ✓	✓ ✓ ✓ ✓ ✓
Cannot ride bikes	✓ ✓ ✓	✓ ✓ ✓ ✓ ✓

How many boys can ride a bike?

How many girls are there altogether?

How many children can't ride bikes?

How many children are there altogether?

Interpreting graphs

Look carefully at the graph and then answer the questions below.

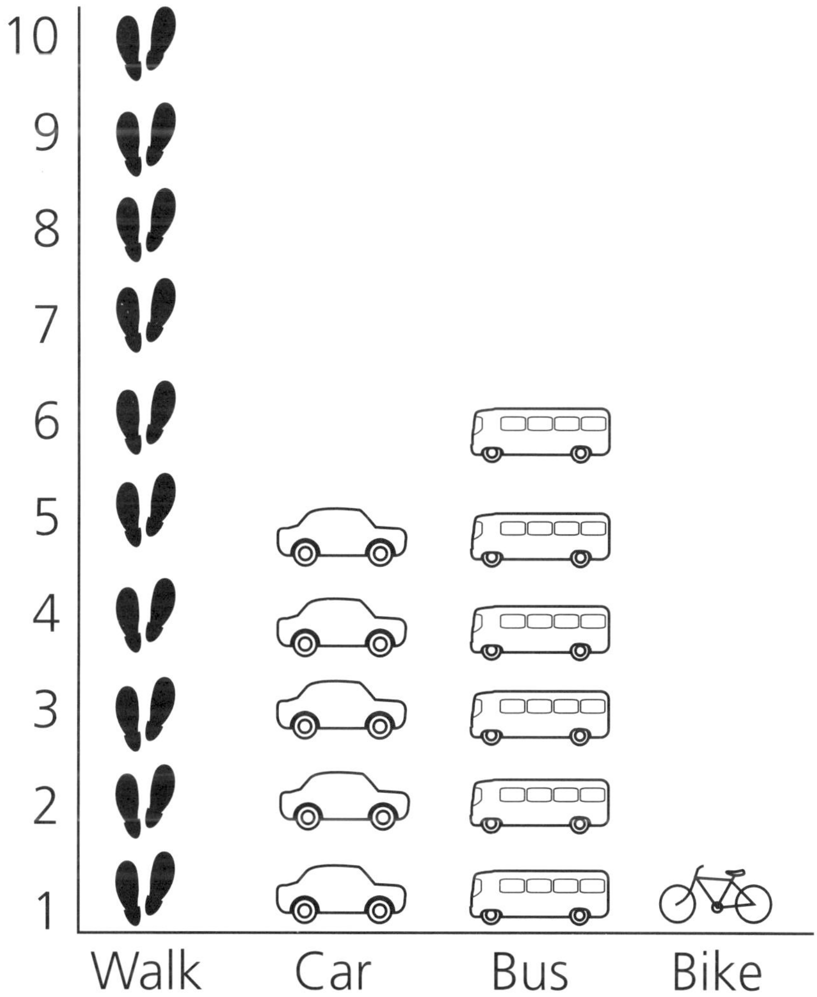

How many children travel to school by bus?

How many more children walk to school than come by car?

How many children are there in the class altogether?

Which way of getting to school is used by only one member of the class?

INDEX